GOD'S
LOVE
IS
FOREVER

—

11-week prayer journal

by Mike Novotny

Published by Straight Talk Books
P.O. Box 301, Milwaukee, WI 53201
800.661.3311 · timeofgrace.org

Printed in the United States of America
ISBN: 978-1-949488-85-2

Give thanks to the LORD, for he is good.
His love endures forever.
Give thanks to the God of gods.
His love endures forever.
Give thanks to the Lord of lords:
His love endures forever.
Give thanks to the God of heaven.
His love endures forever.

Psalm 136:1-3,26

Introduction

The most shocking thing about Jesus might not be his death. I can't imagine his death on a cross—the crown of thorns, the nails, the pain—but what really shocks me is Jesus' life. Because for his entire life, his love endured forever. He didn't run out of love a single time. He never, ever, ever said, "I'm done." He never rolled his eyes at Mary or talked back to Joseph (not even when they told their 12-year-old to do his chores). Jesus loved and then loved and then loved some more, a walking and talking Psalm 136. He obeyed his Father, then obeyed the next day, and then obeyed his whole life. He remembered our sinful situation, our lives filled with temporary love, so he lived for us. Jesus constantly loves for us. His love endures forever. **"Give thanks to the God of heaven. His love endures forever"** (Psalm 136:26).

That means that through faith in Jesus, you get love that endures forever. No matter what fails or sputters or ends, the best part of your life never will—God. The God who can calm your storms, who cares about your anxiety, who controls the economy, who knows every last hair on your head, who's enough for your heart, who's near in your struggles is the same God whose love endures forever.

And that's the beautiful truth behind this prayer journal. So many things in our lives fail us or are temporary, but not Jesus' love.

I hope that the devotions in the pages that follow give

you daily glimpses of God's never-ending love for you. And I pray that the prayer prompts get you started on daily conversations with your Lord and Savior, who loves to hear from you.

There are 11 weeks of devotions and prompts in this journal. Each week begins with a short devotion and a number of general thoughts about your spiritual life. The 6 days that follow seek to unpack the original devotion, line by line, helping you meditate deeply on God's truth and allowing your heart to talk to Jesus about your joys, your fears, your needs, and your wants.

In the end, I hope this journal is a tool that helps you seek God every day as you live your life even now in his presence.

Praying for and with you,

Pastor Mike

*"Never will I leave you;
never will I forsake you."*

Hebrews 13:5

Everything is fleeting, but God's love is forever

For 157 straight Sundays, I wore the same blue, checkered, button-up shirt to church. I'm not exaggerating. A creature of habit I must be, because I loved wearing that shirt. Sadly, the beautiful blue checks started to wear thin, and my treasured church wear ended up in the garbage can.

According to Solomon, that is how life **"under the sun"** works (Ecclesiastes 1:14). All the things of earth, even the things we treasure, are temporary. **"Everything is meaningless,"** Solomon lamented, which was his way of saying that nothing lasts all that long (Ecclesiastes 1:2). Not just clothes, but friends, family, control, praise, productivity, money, and health all come and go, no matter how hard we pray for them to endure. This reality is why we worry so much about tomorrow. We might lose something we love.

This, by contrast, is why I adore God. Our God is eternal. He is everlasting. He endures forever. While anything might leave us and anyone could forsake us, God has promised: **"Never will I leave you; never will I forsake you"** (Hebrews 13:5). The good news is not that God is loving or forgiving or merciful, but that he is eternal. That means his love and forgiveness and mercy endure forever.

In the days to come, I want us to appreciate the eternal nature of God. In a world where everything is fleeting, God's presence is the one thing we can always rely on. That truth is enough to give us true peace.

The part of this devotion that grabs my attention most is . . .

These words make me sorry for . . .

These words make me grateful for . . .

*These words make me
ask for . . .*

*The people I will pray
for this week . . .*

Almighty God,

Date: ___ /___ /___

The last time I lost something that I really loved was . . .

*According to Solomon, that is how life **"under the sun"** works (Ecclesiastes 1:14). All the things of earth, even the things we treasure, are temporary.*

I am tempted to think that some things will last forever, such as . . .

It is healthy for me to know that everything is temporary or else I might . . .

Dear Lord Jesus,

Date: ___ /___ /___

I worry too often about losing . . .

_____
_____
_____
_____
_____
_____
_____
_____
_____
_____
_____

> *Not just clothes,*
> *but friends, family,*
> *comfort, control, praise,*
> *productivity, money, and*
> *health all come and go,*
> *no matter how hard we*
> *pray for them to endure.*
> *This reality is why we*
> *worry so much about*
> *tomorrow. We might lose*
> *something we love.*

It is possible that I love some things too much, such as . . .

_____
_____
_____
_____
_____
_____
_____

If I accepted that everything except God is temporary, I could start to . . .

Jesus, I am so thankful today that, unlike everything and everyone else, you . . .

Holy Spirit,

Date: ___/___/___

God deserves to be adored
because . . .

_____

_____

_____

_____

_____

_____

_____

_____

_____

*This, by contrast,
is why I adore God.
Our God is eternal. He
is everlasting.
He endures forever.*

Other words/phrases that remind me that God is eternal are . . .

_____

_____

_____

_____

_____

_____

_____

If God endures forever, then so does his . . .

The Spirit is helping me adore God even more today by showing me that . . .

Holy Spirit,

Date: ____ / ____ / ____

Today I want to be honest enough to admit that I could lose something wonderful, such as . . .

_____

_____

_____

_____

_____

_____

_____

_____

While anything might leave us and anyone could forsake us, God has promised:
"Never will I leave you; never will I forsake you"
(Hebrews 13:5).

I think God repeated the word never *in this verse because . . .*

_____

_____

_____

_____

_____

_____

_____

Since this promise is true, I can trust that . . .

Someone in my life who really could use this promise is . . .

Almighty God,

Date: ___ /___ /___

If God's love had an expiration date, I would feel . . .

_____

_____

_____

_____

_____

_____

_____

_____

_____

> *The good news is not that God is loving or forgiving or merciful but that he is eternal. That means his love and forgiveness and mercy endure forever.*

The truly unique thing about the God I worship is . . .

_____

_____

_____

_____

_____

_____

_____

My heart craves things that endure forever. That is why I want to seek God today by . . .

My faith is good news today because I believe that . . .

Dear Lord Jesus,

Date: ____ / ____ / ____

I am going to rely on God's presence today by . . .

_____

_____

_____

_____

_____

_____

_____

_____

_____

In a world where everything is fleeting, God's presence is the one thing we can always rely on. That truth is enough to give us true peace.

To me, the word peace means . . .

_____

_____

_____

_____

_____

_____

_____

_____

I am finding myself praying about certain things more lately, such as . . .

This week, God has really been working on my heart to . . .

Holy Spirit,

*"I no longer call you servants,
because a servant does not know
his master's business. Instead, I have
called you friends, for everything
that I learned from my Father
I have made known to you."*

John 15:15

Friendship is fleeting, but God's love is forever

The other day I paged through my grade school yearbooks. Besides the questionable clothing choices and baffling hairstyles, I was struck by a simple fact—I haven't seen those people in years. My dearest friends from those days are now distant memories.

That's how most friendships work, right? Friends come and friends go. You get close and then drift away. The dorm, the job, or the team brings you together, but then the busyness of life pulls you apart. Even friendships that survive the decades are threatened by the grim realities of Alzheimer's and unavoidable funerals.

This, by contrast, is why I adore God. Jesus, God in human flesh, once said, **"I have called you friends"** (John 15:15). Instead of merely being our Savior or King, Jesus is willing to be our friend also. The friend who gets what we're going through (Hebrews 4:15). The friend who cares about our anxiety (1 Peter 5:7). The friend who will be there forever, since he is risen from the grave (Matthew 28:10,20).

I don't know if you have good friends or battle loneliness, but I do know this—Christians are never alone because the eternal God calls us his forever friends.

The part of this devotion that grabs my attention most is . . .

_____

_____

_____

_____

_____

_____

_____

_____

_____

These words make me sorry for . . .

_____

_____

_____

_____

_____

_____

_____

These words make me grateful for . . .

_____

_____

_____

_____

_____

_____

These words make me ask for . . .

_____
_____
_____
_____
_____
_____
_____
_____
_____
_____

The people I will pray for this week . . .

_____
_____
_____
_____
_____
_____
_____
_____
_____
_____

Dear heavenly Father,

_____
_____
_____
_____
_____
_____
_____

Date: ___ / ___ / ___

The names of some of my former friends whom I haven't seen in forever are . . .

_____

_____

_____

_____

_____

_____

_____

My dearest friends from those days are now distant memories. That's how most friendships work, right? Friends come and friends go. You get close and then drift away. The dorm, the job, or the team brings you together, but then the busyness of life pulls you apart.

Some of the biggest reasons that I haven't stayed in touch with old friends are . . .

_____

_____

_____

_____

_____

_____

I love thinking about my relationship with Jesus as a friendship because . . .

Dear heavenly Father,

Date: ___ /___ /___

Even friendships that
survive the decades
are threatened by
the grim realities
of Alzheimer's and
unavoidable funerals.

This sentence is sobering to me
because . . .

A friend I really miss these days is . . .

It is such a comfort to know that my friendship with God will never be in danger because . . .

Holy Spirit,

Date: ___ /___ /___

I am stunned that Jesus would call me his friend because . . .

*Jesus, God in human flesh, once said, "I **have called you friends**" (John 15:15). Instead of merely being our Savior or our King, Jesus is willing to also be our friend.*

The fact that the King of heaven is also my friend means that . . .

A friend of mine who could use this truth today might be . . .

Dear heavenly Father,

Date: ___ /___ /___

A friend who really gets my situation is . . .

[Jesus is] the friend
who gets what
we're going through
(Hebrews 4:15).
The friend who cares
about our anxiety
(1 Peter 5:7).

The fact that Jesus is literally an all-knowing friend makes me feel . . .

Today Jesus wants to help me decrease my anxiety over . . .

Dear Lord Jesus,

Date: ___ / ___ / ___

One of my favorite things about the resurrection of Jesus is . . .

[Jesus is] the friend who will be there forever, since he is risen from the grave (Matthew 28:10,20).

If even death can't stop Jesus from being my friend, then I don't have to fear . . .

The word forever *is such good news because it implies . . .*

Holy Spirit,

Date: ____/____/____

The last time I truly felt lonely was . . .

I don't know if you have good friends or battle loneliness, but I do know this— Christians are never alone because the eternal God calls us his forever friends.

One thing that might help me remember that I'm never alone is . . .

This week I found myself praying most about . . .

The best part of my spiritual life these days is . . .

Dear heavenly Father,

"Well done, good and faithful servant!
You have been faithful with a few things;
I will put you in charge of many things.
Come and share your master's happiness!"

Matthew 25:21

Date: ___ / ___ / ___

Praise is fleeting,
but God's love is forever

I have a special email folder labeled "Encouragement." Whenever a kind, thoughtful word comes my way, I drag that message into that folder, saving it for a rainy day when my critics are many and my motivation is miniscule.

If you've ever been encouraged, you know the emotional power of praise. Perhaps you can even remember the exact words your father or professor or coach spoke to you all those years ago. "Well done, son!" or "You really impressed me!" are sentences that we save in a special folder in our hearts.

The problem, however, is that praise is fleeting. Few people pay attention to our efforts or bother to say anything nice at all. You can work your tail off for months and receive nothing more than your required paycheck. You can change a dozen diapers a day and get zero thanks. You can be a good neighbor, a dedicated volunteer at church, or a selfless spouse and hear crickets (or critiques of what you failed to do well).

This, by contrast, is why I adore God. The eternal God, in sheer mercy, not only forgives us in Christ but dares to praise the good works that we do. Even if our efforts are the smallest things done for the "least of these" on earth, King Jesus will one day shout, **"Well done,"** words that will echo throughout eternity (Matthew 25:21).

So when people forget to praise you (or notice you at all), remember the God who always sees and whose praise endures forever.

The part of this devotion that grabs my attention most is . . .

_____

_____

_____

_____

_____

_____

_____

_____

_____

These words make me sorry for . . .

_____

_____

_____

_____

_____

_____

These words make me grateful for . . .

_____

_____

_____

_____

_____

_____

*These words make me
ask for . . .*

*The people I will pray
for this week . . .*

Dear heavenly Father,

Date: ___ /___ /___

The most memorable thing a family member has ever said to me was . . .

_____

_____

_____

_____

_____

_____

_____

_____

_____

If you've ever been encouraged, you know the emotional power of praise. Perhaps you can even remember the exact words your father or professor or coach spoke to you all those years ago.

The most memorable thing a friend has ever said to me was . . .

_____

_____

_____

_____

_____

_____

_____

_____

The most memorable thing a classmate or coworker has ever said to me was . . .

Recalling these memories makes me feel . . .

The most thrilling thing that God says about me is . . .

Almighty God,

Date: ___ /___ /___

The problem, however, is that praise is fleeting.

I have experienced how fleeting praise is. One time . . .

I need to be careful with how much attention I give to people's praise. Otherwise, I could see myself . . .

One of the connections between this devotion and social media is . . .

By contrast to human praise, my God is . . .

Almighty God,

Date: ___ /___ /___

Few people pay attention to our efforts or bother to say anything nice at all. You can work your tail off for months and receive nothing more than your required paycheck. You can change a dozen diapers a day and get zero thanks. You can be a good neighbor, a dedicated volunteer at church, or a selfless spouse and hear crickets (or critiques of what you failed to do well).

A time I did a great thing and no one praised my efforts was . . .

It was hard when I went the extra mile for . . . and all I heard was . . .

A critic who can really make me lose my joy is . . .

*God, I'm asking for your help
to handle emotionally . . .*

Date: ___ /___ /___

Given how easily I fall apart emotionally, I am so grateful that Jesus . . .

This, by contrast, is why I adore God. The eternal God, in sheer mercy, not only forgives us in Christ but dares to praise the good works that we do.

God praising my efforts must be "sheer mercy" because . . .

It would be enough if Jesus just forgave my sins, but he also . . .

The fact that God would notice and praise my works of faith makes me feel . . .

Almighty God,

Date: ___ / ___ / ___

A small thing that I do out of love for God and others is . . .

> *Even if our efforts are the smallest things done for the "least of these" on earth, King Jesus will one day shout, **"Well done,"** words that will echo throughout eternity (Matthew 25:21).*

One person whom I serve who is not very influential or important is . . .

The fact that Jesus would notice my smallest good work makes me realize that he . . .

_____

_____

_____

_____

Eternal praise from God is better than all the praise of people because . . .

_____

_____

_____

_____

_____

Dear Lord Jesus,

_____

_____

_____

_____

_____

_____

_____

Date: ___ /___ /___

The fact that God always sees
makes me feel . . .

_____

_____

_____

_____

_____

_____

_____

_____

_____

_____

_____

*So when people forget
to praise you (or notice
you at all), remember
the God who always
sees and whose praise
endures forever.*

I am okay with receiving no human praise today because . . .

_____

_____

_____

_____

_____

_____

_____

This week, God was really trying to teach me that . . .

One thing I need the Holy Spirit's help with today is . . .

Holy Spirit,

His love endures forever.
Psalm 136:1

Romance is fleeting, but God's love is forever

As much as I would love to say that the teenage me was saving my heart for Kim (my wife), the truth is that I was romantically pathetic. A six-month-old could have counted how many dates, girlfriends, and total kisses I had before my high school graduation (that is, zero). I learned, the hard way, how uncertain romance is.

That's true for all of us. Meeting "the one" is no guarantee. Convincing that one to commit their life to you is unpredictable too. Even those of us who do exchange vows with the one we love have no idea if that love (or our spouse's life) will last very long. Commitments come and go. Vows are sometimes kept, sometimes broken. Even the best marriages end with one brokenhearted spouse at a funeral.

This, by contrast, is why I adore God. The eternal God vows to give us eternal love. Psalm 136 puts this truth on repeat: **"His love endures forever"** (verses 1 and 2 and 3-26!). Your dating life might be nonexistent, but your God's love endures forever. Your boyfriend might move on, but your God's love endures forever. Your fiancé might get cold feet, but your God's love endures forever. Your wife might grow tired of marriage, but your God's love endures forever. Your beloved husband might pass away, but your God's love endures forever.

When love doesn't last, run to the infinite, bottomless, enduring, and everlasting love of the eternal God.

The part of this devotion that grabs my attention most is . . .

These words make me sorry for . . .

These words make me grateful for . . .

These words make me ask for . . .

The people I will pray for this week . . .

Dear heavenly Father,

Date: ___ / ___ / ___

I think the idea of finding "the one" is spiritually dangerous because . . .

_____
_____
_____
_____
_____
_____
_____
_____

Meeting "the one" is no guarantee. Convincing that one to commit their life to you is unpredictable too.

I know how uncertain relationships can be because I remember . . .

_____
_____
_____
_____
_____
_____
_____

It would be way better to let God be "my one" because . . .

Dear Lord Jesus,

Date: ___ /___ /___

Even those of us who do exchange vows with the one we love have no idea if that love (or our spouse's life) will last for very long. Commitments come and go. Vows are sometimes kept, sometimes broken. Even the best marriages end with one brokenhearted spouse at a funeral.

I know how true these words are when I think about . . .

_____

_____

_____

_____

_____

_____

_____

_____

Personally, I have fallen short of my commitment to others by . . .

_____

_____

_____

_____

_____

_____

_____

_____

These words make me grateful for God by reminding me that . . .

Holy Spirit,

Date: ____ /____ /____

If God's love wasn't enduring, I would feel . . .

The eternal God vows to give us eternal love. Psalm 136 puts this truth on repeat, **"His love endures forever"** (verses 1 and 2 and 3–26!).

I think God repeated "his love endures forever" 26 times in Psalm 136 because . . .

God's never-ending love has the power to . . .

Dear Lord Jesus,

Date: ___ / ___ / ___

"But your God's love . . ."
These words are my rock today
because . . .

_____

_____

_____

_____

_____

_____

_____

_____

_____

*Your dating life might
be nonexistent, but
your God's love endures
forever. Your boyfriend
might move on, but
your God's love endures
forever. Your fiancé
might get cold feet, but
your God's love endures
forever.*

*Although human love might fail me, God's enduring love
changes me by . . .*

_____

_____

_____

_____

_____

_____

A friend who needs these words today is . . .

_____

_____

_____

_____

_____

_____

_____

_____

Almighty God,

_____

_____

_____

_____

_____

_____

_____

_____

_____

_____

Date: ___ / ___ / ___

Jesus didn't need marriage to be content because he knew . . .

Your wife might grow tired of marriage, but your God's love endures forever. Your beloved husband might pass away, but your God's love endures forever.

It is healthy for me to have realistic expectations about relationships because . . .

At the end of every day, I will be loved by God because of Jesus.
These words make me feel . . .

Almighty God,

Date: ___ /___ /___

The word bottomless *makes me think of . . .*

When love doesn't last, run to the infinite, bottomless, enduring, and everlasting love of the eternal God.

Something "enduring" that I can think of is . . .

Meditating on this one sentence helps my heart remember that . . .

This week, I found myself praying often for . . .

Holy Spirit,

"This, then, is how you should pray:
Our Father in heaven, hallowed be your name."

Matthew 6:9

Family is fleeting, but God's love is forever

Pastor Mark Jeske, the original Time of Grace pastor, once told me that I needed to be intentional about parenting in the early teenage years. If memory serves, he said, "Mike, you think you have until they're 18, but you don't. Soon they'll have jobs, friends, and so much going on that you'll barely see them." Pastor Mark encouraged me to make the most of the time I have with my pre-job, pre-car, pre-phone daughters.

Essentially, his words are a reminder of a larger truth—family is fleeting. Some of us want kids but can't find someone to have kids with. Others find that someone but struggle to conceive. Those who are blessed with babies learn, just like *everyone* says, that "they grow up so fast." One day you're packing a diaper bag; the next you're unpacking at their first apartment.

This, by contrast, is why I adore God. The eternal God is the Father of the family that endures forever. Through the death and resurrection of Jesus, we have been gifted a perfect Father, a protective big brother (Jesus), and countless siblings in Christ. In fact, no matter what your biological family life is like, Jesus taught you to pray, **"Our Father . . ."** (Matthew 6:9), a reminder that your spiritual family is forever.

Earthly families, even the best ones, are temporary. Thank God that our Father in heaven is eternal.

The part of this devotion that grabs my attention most is . . .

_____

_____

_____

_____

_____

_____

_____

_____

_____

These words make me sorry for . . .

_____

_____

_____

_____

_____

_____

_____

These words make me grateful for . . .

_____

_____

_____

_____

_____

_____

_____

These words make me ask for . . .

The people I will pray for this week . . .

Dear heavenly Father,

Date: ___ / ___ / ___

One of the hardest things my parents experienced with raising me was . . .

_____

_____

_____

_____

_____

_____

_____

_____

"You think you have until [your kids are] 18, but you don't. Soon they'll have jobs, friends, and so much going on that you'll barely see them."

A kid I have seen grow up "so fast" is . . .

_____

_____

_____

_____

_____

_____

_____

A few things about our modern culture that make this quote especially true are . . .

God's enduring presence is especially important for parents because . . .

— *Dear Lord Jesus,* —

Date: ___ /___ /___

My experience with creating the "perfect family" has been . . .

_____
_____
_____
_____
_____
_____
_____
_____
_____

Family is fleeting. Some of us want kids but can't find someone to have kids with. Others find that someone but struggle to conceive.

Someone who could deeply relate to these words is . . .

_____
_____
_____
_____
_____
_____
_____
_____

One of the hardest things about fertility issues is . . .

I appreciate God's presence when I think about all this because . . .

Dear heavenly Father,

Date: ___ / ___ / ___

When I was young, I thought that time . . .

Those who are blessed with babies learn, just like everyone says, that "they grow up so fast." One day you're packing a diaper bag; the next you're unpacking at their first apartment.

Now that I'm older, I realize that time . . .

If I could go back in time, I think I would . . .

The fact that God is timeless helps me deal with . . .

Almighty God,

Date: ___ /___ /___

> The eternal God is the
> Father of the family
> that endures forever.

God is a lot like my biological father because he . . .

_____
_____
_____
_____
_____
_____
_____
_____
_____

God is a lot unlike my biological father because he . . .

_____
_____
_____
_____
_____
_____
_____

One of my favorite things about having fellow Christians in my life is . . .

Dear heavenly Father,

Date: ___ / ___ / ___

I am grateful for Jesus' death and resurrection today because . . .

Through the death and resurrection of Jesus, we have been gifted a perfect Father, a protective big brother (Jesus), and countless siblings in Christ.

The best thing about having a perfect Father is . . .

Thinking about Jesus as a strong, protective big brother helps me feel more confident about . . .

These particular siblings in Christ have touched my life in these ways . . .

Dear Lord Jesus,

Date: ___ /___ /___

The word *our* in the Lord's Prayer is powerful because . . .

_____
_____
_____
_____
_____
_____
_____
_____
_____
_____
_____

*In fact, no matter what your biological family life is like, Jesus taught you to pray, "**Our Father . . .**" (Matthew 6:9), a reminder that your spiritual family is forever.*

One time that I was blessed by my spiritual family was when . . .

_____
_____
_____
_____
_____
_____
_____
_____

This week, the best moment I had with God was . . .

Dear heavenly Father,

*Christ is the mediator of a new covenant,
that those who are called may receive
the promised eternal inheritance.*

Hebrews 9:15

Money is fleeting,
but God's love is forever

I just made the mistake of looking at my bank statement. $6.85 for bathroom supplies at the grocery store. $0.93 for gas station coffee. $23.73 for new clothes from Kohl's. $114.49 for life/disability insurance. $36.00 for the YMCA. $129.78 for Aldi. Here's the worst part—that list was only *some* of the charges from the last 48 hours!

Money is fleeting. Proverbs remind us: **"Cast but a glance at riches, and they are gone, for they will surely sprout wings and fly off to the sky like an eagle"** (23:5). We work so hard to earn and save money, but then our expenses suck every dollar and cent out of our accounts. One day you have money in the bank; the next you're asking friends to wait before they cash your checks. It's hard, even in the First World, to feel secure about your financial situation.

This, by contrast, is why I adore God. The eternal God has promised his people eternal riches: **"Christ is the mediator of a new covenant, that those who are called may receive the promised eternal inheritance"** (Hebrews 9:15). We have eternal riches that are guaranteed to endure. The promise of God's presence, of greater worth than an armored truck full of gold, is an inheritance that no uninsured driver, company downsizing, or market crash can touch.

In other words, no matter what your net worth or your credit score, you are and always will be spiritually rich. Because God's love endures forever.

The part of this devotion that grabs my attention most is . . .

These words make me sorry for . . .

These words make me grateful for . . .

These words make me ask for . . .

The people I will pray for this week . . .

Dear heavenly Father,

Date: ___ / ___ / ___

A closer look at my checking
account would make me feel . . .

_____

_____

_____

_____

_____

_____

_____

_____

I just made the
mistake of looking at
my bank statement.

One of the things that concerns me about my financial situation
is . . .

_____

_____

_____

_____

_____

_____

I am so grateful for God when I think about money because . . .

Dear Lord Jesus,

Date: ___ /___ /___

I know that money is fleeting because one time . . .

_____

_____

_____

_____

_____

_____

_____

_____

_____

Money is fleeting. Proverbs reminds us: **"Cast but a glance at riches, and they are gone, for they will surely sprout wings and fly off to the sky like an eagle"** (23:5).

The God who loves me only wants me to "glance" at riches because he knows that I tend to . . .

_____

_____

_____

_____

_____

_____

A few things that I am so glad will never "fly off to the sky" are . . .

Holy Spirit,

Date: ___ /___ /___

We work so hard to earn and save money, but then our expenses suck every dollar and cent out of our accounts. One day you have money in the bank; the next you're asking friends to wait before they cash your checks. It's hard, even in the First World, to feel secure about your financial situation.

When I compare my life to the lives of people around the world, I feel . . .

Maybe the reason even rich people worry so much about money is . . .

As much as I think I wouldn't worry if I had more money, the truth is that . . .

Today I would love God to help me with . . .

— Almighty God,

Date: ___ /___ /___

The eternal God has promised his people eternal riches: **"Christ is the mediator of a new covenant, that those who are called may receive the promised eternal inheritance"** (Hebrews 9:15).

The "riches" that Jesus has given me are better than the lottery because . . .

_____

_____

_____

_____

_____

_____

_____

_____

The fact that I am "called" to be with God makes me feel . . .

_____

_____

_____

_____

_____

_____

_____

_____

When I hear about my inheritance from heaven, my mind pictures . . .

Dear heavenly Father,

Date: ___ /___ /___

We have eternal riches that are guaranteed to endure. The promise of God's presence, of greater worth than an armored truck full of gold, is an inheritance that no uninsured driver, company downsizing, or market crash can touch.

When I remember that my treasure is safe in heaven, it makes me worry less about . . .

_____

_____

_____

_____

_____

_____

_____

_____

God's presence is the greatest inheritance on earth because it offers me . . .

_____

_____

_____

_____

_____

_____

_____

One way I could remember these words throughout this week would be to . . .

There are people in my city who are truly needy. Here are some ways I can give of the blessings God has given me . . .

Dear Lord Jesus,

Date: ___ / ___ / ___

I think too much/not enough/ just enough about my credit score because . . .

_____

_____

_____

_____

_____

_____

_____

_____

In other words, no matter what your net worth or your credit score, you are and always will be spiritually rich. Because God's love endures forever.

Thinking more about how spiritually rich I am makes me feel like I can . . .

_____

_____

_____

_____

_____

_____

One friend who needs me to share this message with them is . . .

Jesus is worthy of my worship today because he . . .

Holy Spirit,

We are God's handiwork,
created in Christ Jesus to do good works,
which God prepared in advance for us to do.

Ephesians 2:10

Date: ___/___/___

Productivity is fleeting, but God's love is forever

If you've never met my wife, Kim, you should know that she is a smart, organized, disciplined, humble-but-hardworking, box-checking woman. She loves to get stuff done, a passion that is a HUGE blessing to me, her coworkers, and our children. So when Kim gets stuff done, she is happy. And when life gets in the way of her list, she's not.

That's the frustrating part about life, isn't it? You intend to do this, but then that happens. You have plans to finish up these things, but then those things (or those people) interrupt you. Just when you're in the groove, the phone rings, the emergency email beeps, and the urgent text buzzes. Productivity is always one emergency away from exploding. Even if we get today's list done, there's always another list waiting for us tomorrow.

This, by contrast, is why I adore God. The eternal God always gets his to-do list done. As the all-knowing God, he is never surprised by the events of life. As the all-powerful God, he never runs into a situation he can't take care of.

Paul wrote that the God who saved us by his grace **"created [us] in Christ Jesus to do good works, which God prepared in advance for us to do"** (Ephesians 2:10). God has good works for you to do. They might interrupt your plans for the day, but that's no reason to panic. Just remember that while our productivity is fleeting, God's is perfect. That truth can make all of us, even Kim, extremely happy.

The part of this devotion that grabs my attention most is . . .

_____

_____

_____

_____

_____

_____

_____

_____

_____

These words make me sorry for . . .

_____

_____

_____

_____

_____

_____

_____

These words make me grateful for . . .

_____

_____

_____

_____

_____

_____

_____

These words make me ask for . . .

The people I will pray for this week . . .

Dear heavenly Father,

Date: ___ /___ /___

Something I intended to do by this point in life but didn't get done is . . .

_____

_____

_____

_____

_____

_____

_____

That's the frustrating part about life, isn't it? You intend to do this, but then that happens. You have plans to finish up these things, but then those things (or those people) interrupt you. Just when you're in the groove, the phone rings, the emergency email beeps, and the urgent text buzzes.

On a stress scale of 1 to 10, when life interrupts my plans, I tend to end up at . . . and that usually looks like this . . .

_____

_____

_____

_____

_____

_____

When I am frustrated by a lack of productivity, I tend to . . .

God, when things don't go my way this week, help me remember that . . .

Date: ___/___/___

A recent emergency that messed with my life goals was . . .

_____
_____
_____
_____
_____
_____
_____
_____
_____
_____
_____

Productivity is always one emergency away from exploding. Even if we get today's list done, there is always another list waiting for us tomorrow.

A few reasons why God wants me to strive for productivity are . . .

_____
_____
_____
_____
_____
_____
_____
_____

If I'm not careful with my personal to-do lists, I could foresee . . .

Dear Lord Jesus,

Date: ____ /____ /____

I have seen God work through uncertain times, like when . . .

_____

_____

_____

_____

*The eternal God
always gets his
to-do list done.*

_____

_____

_____

_____

_____

*A few of God's qualities that ensure he always accomplishes his
purposes are . . .*

_____

_____

_____

_____

_____

_____

If I had to guess how much of my to-do list matches up with God's plans for me, it would be . . .

What brings me the most comfort from today's words is . . .

Holy Spirit,

Date: ____ /____ /____

One of the things that is stressing me out that God has under his total control is . . .

_____
_____
_____
_____
_____
_____
_____
_____
_____

As the all-knowing God, he is never surprised by the events of life. As the all-powerful God, he never runs into a situation he can't take care of.

If I could remember that God knows, God cares, and God can, my life might look like . . .

_____
_____
_____
_____
_____
_____
_____

It's okay if I don't achieve all my goals for this week because God could . . . or he could . . . or he could . . .

Almighty God,

Date: ___ /___ /___

"God saved us by his grace."
That short sentence makes me
feel . . .

Paul wrote that the
God who saved us by
his grace **"created** [us]
**in Christ Jesus to do
good works, which
God prepared in
advance for us to do"**
(Ephesians 2:10).

_____

_____

_____

_____

_____

_____

_____

_____

I was saved to do good works. One of the reasons this inspires
me is . . .

_____

_____

_____

_____

_____

_____

The God who knows every twist and turn of life already prepared my to-do list. One of the ways I could remember this would be to . . .

Dear heavenly Father,

Date: ___ /___ /___

With God, I have no reason to panic the next time that . . .

_____

_____

_____

_____

_____

_____

_____

_____

_____

_____

God has good works for you to do. They might interrupt your plans for the day, but that's no reason to panic. Just remember that while our productivity is fleeting, God's is perfect.

This week has taught me to see life's "interruptions" in a different light by . . .

_____

_____

_____

_____

_____

_____

_____

A friend who could remind me of these words this week would be ...

Recently, the most frequent Bible truth/passage on my mind has been ...

Dear Lord Jesus,

*Jesus Christ is the same yesterday
and today and forever.*

Hebrews 13:8

Success is fleeting, but God's love is forever

One of the worst parts about being a middle-aged runner in the 21st century is that you know you're getting slower. Thanks to the data on my running app, I have objective data to prove that I'm slowing down. It's very possible that my greatest athletic success is completely in the past.

The temporary nature of success is a frustrating part of life, isn't it? We never truly know if our grades will get better (or worse), if our church will need extra chairs (or have enough pew space for people to lie down), or if our business will make money (or close its doors). Success is fleeting, uncertain, and anything but guaranteed. This can be a hard truth to swallow as you enter the final decades of life.

This, by contrast, is why I adore God. The eternal God never has to live off his past success. No, God was glorious to Moses, Isaiah, and John in the past; is glorious to every soul who seeks him in the present; and will be glorious to every eye that sees him in the future. **"Jesus Christ is the same yesterday and today and forever"** (Hebrews 13:8).

That is gloriously good news. The best part of our lives—being with God, not earthly success—is the one thing that will never change. Yes, the young runner might pass us by, the old ways of business might not work, and our church's biggest attendance might already be in the books; but with Jesus we still have a thrilling future because our God is forever!

The part of this devotion that grabs my attention most is . . .

These words make me sorry for . . .

These words make me grateful for . . .

These words make me ask for . . .

The people I will pray for this week . . .

Almighty God,

Date: ___ /___ /___

An area of life where I really want to be successful is . . .

_____

_____

_____

_____

_____

_____

_____

_____

We never truly know if our grades will get better (or worse), if our church will need extra chairs (or have enough pew space for people to lie down), or if our business will make money (or close its doors).

So far, my experience of success in that area has been . . .

_____

_____

_____

_____

_____

_____

_____

A few realistic factors that might prevent my success in life might be . . .

Yet I have a glorious and certain future because . . .

— *Dear Lord Jesus,* —

Date: ___ /___ /___

An example of bitter
disappointment I have seen
in an older person is . . .

_Success is fleeting,
uncertain, and anything
but guaranteed. This
can be a hard truth to
swallow as you enter
the final decades of life._

The final decades of my life could be filled with hope and joy if I
focused my attention on . . .

Some of the guarantees with God that give me immense comfort are . . .

Holy Spirit,

Date: ___ /___ /___

> The eternal God never
> has to live off his past
> success. No, God was
> glorious to Moses,
> Isaiah, and John in
> the past; is glorious to
> every soul who seeks
> him in the present;
> and will be glorious
> to every eye that sees
> him in the future.

A few examples of God's glory
that I can recall from the Bible
are . . .

_____

_____

_____

_____

_____

_____

_____

_____

_____

_____

To me, "seeking God" means . . .

_____

_____

_____

_____

_____

_____

_____

The fact that no matter how many failures I experience in this life I will see God's face in the future makes me feel . . .

Almighty God,

Date: ___ /___ /___

In my past, Jesus proved his love for me by . . .

_____

_____

_____

_____

_____

"Jesus Christ is the same yesterday and today and forever"
(Hebrews 13:8).

_____

_____

_____

_____

Already today, Jesus proved his love for me by . . .

_____

_____

_____

_____

_____

_____

_____

Something Jesus has guaranteed to give me tomorrow (and forever!) is . . .

Dear heavenly Father,

Date: ___ /___ /___

The reason that being with God is the best part of my life is . . .

_____

_____

_____

_____

The best part of our lives—being with God, not earthly success— is the one thing that will never change.

_____

_____

_____

_____

_____

_____

The next time God blesses me with earthly success, I want to re-member that . . .

_____

_____

_____

_____

_____

_____

Someone I know who is dealing with bitter disappointment and could use this message is . . .

Holy Spirit,

Date: ___ / ___ / ___

My future is indeed thrilling because . . .

> *Yes, the young runner might pass us by, the old ways of business might not work, and our church's biggest attendance might already be in the books; but with Jesus we still have a thrilling future because our GOD is forever!*

_____

_____

_____

_____

_____

_____

_____

_____

When I try to imagine what heaven will be like, I think . . .

_____

_____

_____

_____

_____

_____

_____

One part of my spiritual life that I really want to work on this week is . . .

I am especially grateful for the cross today because . . .

Almighty God,

*Be strong in the Lord
and in his mighty power.*

Ephesians 6:10

Health is fleeting, but God's love is forever

Unless my doctor is lying to me, my body isn't getting any better. My 6'3" frame has compressed to 6'2" (on a good day), a bad sign for my curling spine. The jokes about how atrociously I eat yet how impressive my cholesterol is are no longer quite as funny now that the cholesterol is a concern. And here's the kicker—this week I strained a back muscle . . . playing ping-pong!

Have you been there? Are you living proof of Paul's belief that our bodies are in **"bondage to decay"** (Romans 8:21)? Do your joints find it harder to wake up in the morning? Has your mind given up its ability to memorize names, faces, and Bible passages? Do you need "readers" to unfuzz these words or hearing aids to grasp the pastor's message? Age, in a thousand ways, is our enemy.

This, by contrast, is why I adore God. The eternal God who flexed his muscle at the Red Sea and had the power to raise his Son from the grave still has enough strength to fight against your every spiritual enemy. There is no challenge you're facing, no temptation you're denying, and no demon you're resisting that he's not strong enough to overcome.

Paul urges us, **"Be strong in the Lord and in his mighty power"** (Ephesians 6:10). So don't fret if age is taking its toll on you. Your strength will never fade if your strength is the eternal God.

The part of this devotion that grabs my attention most is . . .

These words make me sorry for . . .

These words make me grateful for . . .

These words make me ask for . . .

The people I will pray for this week . . .

Dear heavenly Father,

Date: ____ /____ /____

This year, my body has been frail in these ways . . .

_____

_____

_____

_____

_____

_____

_____

_____

_____

*Are you living proof of Paul's belief that our bodies are in **"bondage to decay"** (Romans 8:21)?*

The word bondage *is Paul's way of saying that . . .*

_____

_____

_____

_____

_____

_____

_____

When I listen to friends and family who are 15 years older than me, I humbly have to admit that . . .

Dear Lord Jesus,

Date: ___ /___ /___

One of the things about my life that is getting harder is . . .

_____

_____

_____

_____

_____

_____

_____

_____

Do your joints find it harder to wake up in the morning? Has your mind given up its ability to memorize names, faces, and Bible passages? Do you need "readers" to unfuzz these words or hearing aids to grasp the pastor's message?

If I could regain one part of my youth it would be . . .

_____

_____

_____

_____

_____

_____

_____

God's faithfulness to older people is a great comfort to me because . . .

_____

_____

_____

_____

_____

_____

_____

_____

Almighty God,

_____

_____

_____

_____

_____

_____

_____

_____

_____

Date: ___ / ___ / ___

One of my favorite memories of God using his strength to bless me is . . .

The eternal God who flexed his muscle at the Red Sea and had the power to raise his Son from the grave still has enough strength to fight against your every spiritual enemy.

One of my favorite stories of God using his strength to bless his people is . . .

A few spiritual enemies that are trying to take away my joy today are . . .

The resurrection of Jesus helps me today by reminding me that . . .

Dear heavenly Father,

Date: ___ /___ /___

A challenge I am facing right now is . . .

_____

_____

_____

_____

_____

_____

_____

_____

_____

There is no challenge you're facing, no temptation you're denying, and no demon you're resisting that he's not strong enough to overcome.

A temptation I am struggling against right now is . . .

_____

_____

_____

_____

_____

_____

_____

_____

A demonic lie that I believe too often is . . .

The fact that Jesus is stronger than my strongest enemies makes me . . .

Holy Spirit,

Date: ____ /____ /____

I want to put my strength in
the Lord today because . . .

Paul urges us, **"Be
strong in the Lord and
in his mighty power"**
(Ephesians 6:10).

The fact that God has "mighty power" encourages me to believe
that . . .

One of the ways I could be strong in the Lord today would be to . . .

Almighty God,

Date: ___ /___ /___

It's okay if I'm getting older and weaker because . . .

So don't fret if age is taking its toll on you. Your strength will never fade if your strength is the eternal God.

Putting my strength in the eternal God this week would look like . . .

An elderly person I could share this message with might be . . .

What I appreciate most about God these days is . . .

Dear heavenly Father,

Be still, and know that I am God.

Psalm 46:10

Comfort is fleeting, but God's love is forever

"Can I put on my comfies?" That question is asked nearly every night in my home. When Kim or I come home from work, we ache for that moment when we can change out of the teacher/pastor clothes and put on the stretchy pants and fuzzy sweatshirts. Few things feel better than feeling comfortable.

One of the problems with life is that it's rarely comfortable. From uncomfortable shoes to uncomfortable situations to uncomfortable conversations, it's rare that we can truly relax and let things go. If Jesus called people to **"take up their cross"** and follow him, we probably shouldn't expect a stretchy-pants kind of life (Mark 8:34).

This, by contrast, is why I adore God. Because God is offering us eternal comfort. One day, very soon, Jesus will return, and every uncomfortable moment will be over. The discomfort of death will pass. The wincing of pain will be gone too. The reign of discomfort will end, and Jesus will make all things new (Revelation 21:4,5). Even now, our Savior invites us to **"be still, and know that I am God"** (Psalm 46:10).

Can you even fathom it? When we see Jesus, we will put on eternal comfort, happiness that will never end. Bodily aches and relational pains will be locked in the past. Our forever future will be one of rest, relaxation, and indescribable comfort. Few things—not even stretchy pants—could feel better than that!

The part of this devotion that grabs my attention most is . . .

_____

_____

_____

_____

_____

_____

_____

_____

_____

These words make me sorry for . . .

_____

_____

_____

_____

_____

_____

_____

These words make me grateful for . . .

_____

_____

_____

_____

_____

_____

_____

These words make me ask for . . .

The people I will pray for this week . . .

Dear heavenly Father,

Date: ___ /___ /___

One of the problems with life is that it's rarely comfortable. From uncomfortable shoes to uncomfortable situations to uncomfortable conversations, it's rare that we can truly relax and let things go.

Some of the more uncomfortable things about my life right now are . . .

_____

_____

_____

_____

_____

_____

_____

I find it really hard to relax when . . .

_____

_____

_____

_____

_____

_____

_____

_____

Jesus allows me to let things go today because he . . .

Dear Lord Jesus,

Date: ___ / ___ / ___

*If Jesus called people to **"take up their cross"** and follow him, we probably shouldn't expect a stretchy-pants kind of life (Mark 8:34).*

Taking up my cross for Jesus might mean that I have to give up . . .

_____

_____

_____

_____

_____

_____

_____

_____

_____

From what I know about Jesus' closest friends in the Bible, following Christ might cost me . . .

_____

_____

_____

_____

_____

_____

A few reasons why I believe that Jesus is worth suffering for are . . .

Dear Lord Jesus,

Date: ___ /___ /___

When Jesus comes back, I imagine that I will . . .

_____
_____
_____
_____
_____
_____
_____
_____
_____
_____

God is offering us eternal comfort. One day, very soon, Jesus will return, and every uncomfortable moment will be over. The discomfort of death will pass. The wincing of pain will be gone too.

The discomfort that I can't wait for Jesus to end once and for all is . . .

_____
_____
_____
_____
_____
_____
_____

Being free from the possibility of pain is one of eternity's greatest joys. Some other promises that encourage me today are . . .

Almighty God,

Date: ____ / ____ / ____

I can't wait to see what happens when Jesus changes . . .

_____

_____

_____

_____

_____

_____

_____

_____

_____

*The reign of discomfort will end, and Jesus will make all things new (Revelation 21:4,5). Even now, our Savior invites us to **"be still, and know that I am God"** (Psalm 46:10).*

For me to "be still" today would take . . .

_____

_____

_____

_____

_____

_____

_____

One of the ways for me to remember that "he is God" would be . . .

The person whom I'd like to share this psalm verse with today is . . .

— *Dear heavenly Father,*

Date: ____ /____ /____

When I see Jesus, I think I will say . . .

_____

_____

_____

_____

_____

_____

_____

_____

_____

When we see Jesus, we will put on eternal comfort, happiness that will never end. Bodily aches and relational pains will be locked in the past.

The closest I have been to this kind of happiness was when . . .

_____

_____

_____

_____

_____

_____

_____

Jesus, I want to thank you today for . . .

Date: ___/___/___

My favorite part about "rest" is . . .

_____

_____

_____

_____

_____

_____

_____

_____

_____

Our forever future will be one of rest, relaxation, and indescribable comfort.

I know that I can relax in God's presence because . . .

_____

_____

_____

_____

_____

_____

_____

_____

The closest I could come to describing the comfort of heaven would be . . .

This week, I am humbled when I think about . . .

Holy Spirit,

*But our citizenship is in heaven.
And we eagerly await a Savior from there,
the Lord Jesus Christ, who, by the power that
enables him to bring everything under
his control, will transform our lowly bodies
so that they will be like his glorious body.*

Philippians 3:20,21

Control is fleeting,
but God's love is forever

I learned from a local doctor how common it is for teenage girls to cut themselves. Self-harm might seem like odd behavior, but the doctor's reasoning made sense: "They want something they can control." Many young women are dealing with parents they can't control (will they divorce?) and a future they can't control (will the college accept me?), so they turn to something they have total control of.

I've never been tempted to self-harm in that way, but I do understand the frustration of feeling out of control. I like to fix things, and when I seem incapable of fixing a problem, it bothers me immensely.

Do you lose sleep thinking about the things you can't control? In a broken world, our fleeting ability to control things is frustrating.

This, by contrast, is why I adore God. The apostle Paul once said of our Savior, **"By the power that enables him to bring everything under his control . . ."** (Philippians 3:21). Note the word "everything." There is nothing you are dealing with that's out of Jesus' grasp. Instead of turning to self-harm, we can turn ourselves to the Holy One who has everything under his control. Whether it's wonderful or painful, Jesus has your whole world in his hands and uses it to draw you closer to God.

There's no reason to fear, no matter how helpless you feel. The eternal God has things completely under control.

The part of this devotion that grabs my attention most is . . .

These words make me sorry for . . .

These words make me grateful for . . .

These words make me ask for . . .

The people I will pray for this week . . .

Dear Lord Jesus,

Date: ___ /___ /___

I think so many people these days are turning to destructive habits because . . .

_____

_____

_____

_____

Self-harm might seem like odd behavior, but the doctor's reasoning made sense: "They want something they can control."

_____

_____

_____

_____

When I feel like things are out of my control, I tend to . . .

_____

_____

_____

_____

_____

_____

_____

Knowing that God has the whole world in his hands allows me to . . .

_____

_____

_____

_____

_____

_____

_____

_____

_____

Dear Lord Jesus,

_____

_____

_____

_____

_____

_____

_____

_____

_____

_____

_____

Date: ____ / ____ / ____

A few problems that I am incapable of fixing right now are . . .

_____

_____

_____

_____

_____

_____

_____

_____

I like to fix things, and when I seem incapable of fixing a problem, it bothers me immensely. How about you?

When faced with an unfixable situation, I . . .

_____

_____

_____

_____

_____

_____

_____

Remembering that God is both full of power and full of love for me will help me to . . .

Holy Spirit,

Date: ___ / ___ / ___

I love the word everything *in this verse because it . . .*

The apostle Paul once said of our Savior, **"By the power that enables him to bring everything under his control . . ."** *(Philippians 3:21).*

If I kept repeating "God's got this!" I finally might be able to start . . .

A family member whom I should share this verse with is . . . and he/she needs to hear it because . . .

Almighty God,

Date: ___ / ___ / ___

Two things I really wish I didn't have to deal with right now are . . .

There's nothing you're dealing with that's out of Jesus' grasp.

Knowing that Jesus' scarred hands are holding me helps because . . .

Four things going on in the world right now that are under Jesus' control are . . .

Dear Lord Jesus,

Date: ____/____/____

Turning myself to the Holy One today would look like . . .

Instead of turning to self-harm, we can turn ourselves to the Holy One who has everything under his control. Whether it's wonderful or painful, Jesus has your whole world in his hands and uses it to draw you closer to God.

The word your *in that final sentence is incredibly comforting because . . .*

God might be using the challenges I am facing to bless me by . . .

Dear heavenly Father,

Date: ____ / ____ / ____

Despite this week's devotion,
I am still slightly afraid of . . .

_____
_____
_____
_____
_____
_____
_____
_____
_____
_____

> *There's no reason to fear, no matter how helpless you feel. The eternal God has things completely under control.*

But the fact that God is in control and God is eternal is the perfect solution because . . .

_____
_____
_____
_____
_____
_____
_____

One thing I want to pray throughout the rest of today is . . .

This book has drawn me closer to God by . . .

Holy Spirit,

About the Writer

Pastor Mike Novotny pours his Jesus-based joy into his ministry as a pastor at The CORE (Appleton, Wisconsin) and as the lead speaker for Time of Grace, a global media ministry that connects people to God through television, print, and digital resources. Unafraid to bring grace and truth to the toughest topics of our time, he has written numerous books, including 3 *Words That Will Change Your Life*; *What's Big Starts Small*; *You Know God Loves You, Right?*; and *When Life Hurts*. Mike lives with his wife, Kim, and their two daughters, Brooklyn and Maya; runs long distances; and plays soccer with other middle-aged men whose best days are long behind them. To find more books by Pastor Mike, go to timeofgrace.store.

About Time of Grace

Time of Grace is for people who are experiencing the highest of highs or have hit rock bottom or are anywhere in between. That's because through Time of Grace, you will be reminded that the One who can help you in your life, the God of forgiveness and grace and mercy, is not far away. He is right here with you. GOD is here! He will help you on your spiritual journey. Walk with us at timeofgrace.org.

**To discover more, please visit
timeofgrace.org or call 800.661.3311.**

Help share God's
message of grace!

Every gift you give helps Time of Grace reach people around the world with the good news of Jesus. Your generosity and prayer support take the gospel of grace to others through our ministry outreach and help them experience a satisfied life as they see God all around them.

**Give today at timeofgrace.org/give
or by calling 800.661.3311.**

Thank you!

High Fiber

You will never get
the truth out of a
narcissist. The
closest you will ever
come is a story
that either makes
them the victim or
the hero, but
never the villain.

Almonds   oats
apples   pears
Bananas   sweet
Berries   pot.
Broccoli   brown
carrots   Rice